MW00513064

Easy Air Fryer Cookbook

Easy and Affordable Recipes for Beginners on a Budget. Mouth-watering, Easy to make, Healthy and Tasty Recipes to Burn Fat, Stop Hypertension and Cut Cholesterol.

Brenda Loss

Table of Contents

Introduction

The air fryer is an innovative way to cook food that is both healthy and easy. The air fryer ensures healthy food without using too much oil. Instead of oil, this remarkable kitchen appliance uses circulating hot air to cook food. The method is fast, convenient, and can be surprisingly good, but only if you are equipped with the right recipes. This air fryer cookbook is comprised of a delicious collection of recipes that are suitable for all tastes. Each recipe is full of flavor, simple to make, and offers a healthier alternative to traditionally cooked foods. This air fryer cookbook is filled with recipes for delicious, crispy delights. The air fryer can create fried food fast without added fat, calories, or guilt.

Your air fryer can cook more than fried foods. You can also bake, grill, and roast with your air fryer. Besides recipes, this cookbook includes tips and tricks to help you get the most out of your air fryer. You are guaranteed to find a wonderful selection of traditional, modern, and alternative recipes to suit any palette. With the help of this cookbook, dive into the variety of delicious air fryer recipes that will be good for your taste buds, stomach, body, and soul. Break out your air fryer and enjoy all the great recipes at your fingertips. Your entire family will love each and every one! Get a copy of this air fryer cookbook with 100 selected recipes for easy, no-fuss meals!

CHAPTER 1:

What is an Air Fryer?

An air fryer is a kitchen appliance that cooks food by circulating super-hot air around the food giving it that beautiful crunch without actually using oil for frying. The crunchy layer which we just mentioned that adheres the surface of any deep fried food, is due to the 'Maillard effect'.

Very little to mere spraying of oil can still be used to get the traditional essence of any food. Moreover all the cooking units of an air fryer are lined with a non-stick coating. So, even without oil, everything is just fine. Most air fryers come with adjustable temperature and timer knobs for convenient and customized cooking. Who doesn't like French Fries but everyone knows the amount of oil it has. Also health conscious people tend to keep a distance from any oily food. But if I tell you that you can have all the Fried food yet keep your oil meter in check sounds fishy? Not in the 21st century, Behold the power of Air Fryer. The Air fryer can reduce oil usage by more than 75%. You can also use no oil if you want to and yet the food tastes great. So,have your fries, chips, chicken wings and still stay well within your daily calorie goals.

CHAPTER 2:

Benefits of The Air Fryer

Reduces fat content: One-reason air fryers are better than deep fryers is the fact that they help cut down on fat. When you deep-fry your meals, the fat content in your food is very high because it requires immersing your food in oil. However, air fryers allow you to fry your food with little oil. This helps to reduce the fat content in your meal.

Helps you lose weight: Air fryers are really good for weight loss. Aside from lowering the fat content in your meal, air fryers also help you reduce your calorie intake. The air fryer requires very little oil to make your food crispy and crunchy, thereby reducing your calorie intake. When deep-frying food in oil, we add many calories, so one of the most attractive benefits of an air fryer is the reduction of these extra calories.

Much healthier than deep-fried foods: If you desire to eat healthy meals, join the number of people who have made air-fryer meals their lifestyle.

Reduction of energy expenditure: If you compare the energy consumption of the air fryer with that of a standard electric oven, you can see consumption varies by a reasonably high percentage. You can save more than 50% of electrical energy when using the fryer. For example, the air fryer consumes about 390Wh to fry a pound of potatoes, 45% less electricity than a conventional oven uses.

Saving money: You use less oil, and you need less energy when cooking with an air fryer. So you save money.

CHAPTER 3:

Components of the Air fryer

Any air fryer has the following detachable parts:
Cover (main body).
• Basket holder.
• Divider.
• Basket.

The base of the appliance is the cover or the main body which has the actual functioning unit. Above which there's the basket holder which holds the cooking basket. It has the mechanical fan installed beneath it (this may vary with brands).
Up furthermore, there is the cooking basket where the food is supposed to be kept for cooking.

CHAPTER 4:

Function Keys

Button / Play/Pause Button
•This Play/Pause button allows you to pause during the middle of the cooking so you can shake the air fryer basket or flip the food to ensure it cooks evenly.

-/+ Button /Minus/Plus Button
•This button is used to change the time or temperature.

Food Presets
•This button gives you the ability to cook food without second-guessing. The time and temperature are already set, so new users find this setting useful.

Roast or Broil
•You can roast or broil with this setting. When using a conventional oven, you need to brown the meat before roasting. You can skip this step when cooking with an air fryer.

Keep Warm
•This function keeps your food warm for 30 minutes.

CHAPTER 5:

Features

Temperature and Timer

Avoid the waiting time for your fryer to decide when it wants to heat up. With an air fryer, once you power it on, the fryer will instantly heat. When using the appliance cold, that is, right after it has been off for a while (since last use) all you have to do is add three minutes to your cooking time to allow for it to heat up properly. The appliance is equipped with an adjustable temperature control that allows you to set the temperature that can be altered for each of your meals. Most fryers can go up all the way up to 200-300 degrees. Because the fryer can cook food at record times, it comes with a timer that can be pre-set with no more than 30 minutes. You can even check on the progress of your foods without messing up the set time. Simply pull out the pan, and the fryer will pause heating. When you replace the pan, heating will resume. When your meal is prepared and your timer runs out, the fryer will alert you with its ready sound indicator. But just in-case you can't make it to the fryer when the timer goes, the fryer will automatically switch off to help prevent your ingredients from overcooking and burning.

Food Separator

Some air fryers are supplied with a food separator that enables you to prepare multiple meals at once. For example, if you wanted to prepare frozen chicken nuggets and french fries, you could use the separator to cook both ingredients at the same time, all the while avoiding the worry of the flavors mixing. An air fryer is perfect for quick and easy, lunch and dinner combinations. It is recommended to pair similar ingredients together when using the separator. This will allow both foods to share a similar temperature setting.

Air Filter

Some air fryers are built with an integrated air filter that eliminates those unwanted vapors and food odors from spreading around your house.

No more smelling like your favorite fried foods, the air filter will diffuse that hot oil steam that floats and sticks. You can now enjoy your fresh kitchen smell before, during and after using your air fryer.

Cleaning

No need to fret after using an air fryer, it was designed for hassle-free cleaning. The parts of the fryer are constructed of non-stick material. This prevents any food from sticking to surfaces that ultimately make it hard to clean. It is recommended to soak the parts of the appliances before cleaning. All parts such as the grill, pan and basket are removable and dishwasher friendly. After your ingredients are cooked to perfection, you can simply place your parts in the dishwasher for a quick and easy clean.

For all that they can do, air fryers can definitely be worth the cost. It has been highly questionable if the benefits of an air fryer are worth the expense. When you weigh your pros and cons, the air fryer surely leads with its pros. There aren't many fryers on the market that can fry, bake, grill and roast; and also promise you healthier meals.

An air fryer saves you time, and could potentially save you money. Whether the air fryer is cost effective for your life, is ultimately up to you.

CHAPTER 6:

Safety Tips

1. Do not buy a cheap, low-quality air fryer.

2. Do not place it on an uneven surface.

3. Do not overcrowd the basket.

4. Do not leave the appliance unattended.

5. Read the air fryer manual before using it.

6. Clean the appliance after every use.

7. Do not wash the electrical components.

8. Dry your hands before touching the air fryer.

9. Make sure accessories are air fryer safe.

10. Use the right amount of oil. Your air fryer needs only a little oil

11. If your air fryer needs repairing, seek professional support.

12. Shake the basket or flip the food during the middle of the cooking to ensure even cooking.

CHAPTER 7:

Step By Step Guidelines

Air fryers work on Rapid Air Technology. The cooking chamber of the air fryer emits heat from a heating element that is close to the food. The exhaust fan that is present above the cooking chamber aids in the necessary airflow from the underside. For cooking using an air fryer, here are some steps that you need to follow:

Prepare Fried Foods:

Place the air fryer on a level and heatproof kitchen top. Prepare the foods.

Grease the basket with a little oil and add a bit more to the food to avoid sticking.

If the food is marinated, pat it dry lightly to prevent splattering and excess smoke.

Use aluminum foil for easy cleaning.

Before Cooking:

Preheat the air fryer for 3 minutes before cooking.

Avoid overcrowding and leave sufficient space for air circulation.

During Cook Time:

Add water into the air fryer drawer to prevent excessive smoke and heat

Shake the basket or flip the food for even cooking at the halfway mark.

CHAPTER 8:

Troubleshooting & FAQ

Troubleshooting

Food not cooking perfectly: Follow the recipe exactly. Check whether or not you have overcrowded the ingredients. This is the main reason why food might not cook evenly in an air fryer.

White smoke: White smoke is usually the result of grease, so make sure that you have added some water to the bottom drawer to prevent the grease from overheating.

Black smoke: Black smoke is usually due to burnt food. You need to clean the air fryer after every use. If you do not, then the remaining food particles are burned when you use the appliance again. Turn the machine off and cool it completely. Then check it for burned food.

The appliance won't stop: The fan of the air fryer operates at high speed and needs some time to stop. Do not worry, it will stop soon.

FAQ

1. Can I cook different foods in the air fryer?

Yes, you can cook different foods in your air fryer. You can use it for cooking different types of foods like casseroles and even desserts.

2. How much food can I put inside?

Different air fryers tend to have different capacities. To know how much food you can put in, look for the "max" mark and use it as a guide to filling the basket.

Yes, you can use both to line the base of the air fryer. However, make sure that you poke holes so that the hot air can pass through the material and allow the food to cook.

COOKING - BAKING conversions

WEIGHT

IMPERIAL	METRIC
1/2 oz	15 g
1 oz	29 g
2 oz	57 g
3 oz	85 g
4 oz	113 g
5 oz	141 g
6 oz	170 g
8 oz	227 g
10 oz	283 g
12 oz	340 g
13 oz	369 g
14 oz	397 g
15 oz	425 g
1 lb	453 g

MEASUREMENT

CUP	ONCES	MILLILITERS	TBSP
1/16	1/2 oz	15 ml	1
1/8	1 oz	30 ml	3
1/4	2 oz	59 ml	4
1/3	2.5 oz	79 ml	5.5
3/8	3 oz	90 ml	6
1/2	4 oz	118 ml	8
2/3	5 oz	158 ml	11
3/4	6 oz	177 ml	12
1	8 oz	240 ml	16
2	16 oz	480 ml	32
4	32 oz	960 ml	64
5	40 oz	1180 ml	80
6	48 oz	1420 ml	96
8	64 oz	1895 ml	128

TEMPERATURE

FAHRENHEIT	CELSIUS
100 °F	37 °C
150 °F	65 °C
200 °F	93 °C
250 °F	121 °C
300 °F	150 °C
325 °F	160 °C
350 °F	180 °C
375 °F	190 °C
400 °F	200 °C
425 °F	220 °C
450 °F	230 °C
500 °F	260 °C
525 °F	274 °C
550 °F	288 °C

CHAPTER 9:

Breakfast & Brunch

1.   Bread Rolls With Potato Stuffing

Servings Provided: 4

Ingredients :

Bread - white part only (8 slices)

Potatoes (5 large)

Oil - frying and brushing (2 tbsp.)

Finely chopped coriander (1 small bunch)

Seeded and finely chopped green chilies (2)

Turmeric (.5 tsp.)

Curry leaf sprigs (2)

Mustard seeds (.5 tsp.)

Finely chopped small onions (2)

Salt (as desired)

Directions :

1. Set the Air Fryer at 392° Fahrenheit.

2. Remove the edges of the bread. Peel the potatoes and boil. Mash the potatoes using one teaspoon of salt.

3. On the stovetop, prepare a skillet using one teaspoon of oil. Toss in the mustard seeds and onions. When the seeds sputter, continue frying until they become translucent. Toss in the curry and turmeric.

4. Fry the mixture a few seconds and add the mashed potatoes. Mix well and let it cool. Shape eight portions of dough into an oval shape. Set them aside for now.

5. Wet the bread with water and press it in your palm to remove the excess water. Place the oval potato into the bread and roll it around the potato mixture. Be sure they are completely sealed.

6. Brush the potato rolls with oil and set aside.

7. Set the timer for 12 to 13 minutes. Cook until crispy and browned.

2.   Cheesy Garlic Bread

Servings Provided: 3-4

Ingredients :

Bread slices - Round or baguette (5 rounds)

Sun-dried tomato pesto (5 tsp.)

Garlic cloves (3)

Melted butter (4 tbsp.)

Grated Mozzarella cheese (1 cup)

Garnish Options:

Chili flakes

Chopped basil leaves

Oregano

Directions :

1. Set the Air Fryer to reach 356° Fahrenheit.
2. Slice the bread loaf into five thick slices.
3. Spread the butter, pesto, and cheese over the bread.
4. Put the slices in the Air Fryer for six to eight minutes.
5. Garnish with your choice of toppings.
6. Note: Round or baguette bread was used for this recipe.

3.   Quick & Easy Poached Eggs

Servings Provided: 1

Ingredients :

Boiling water (3 cups)

Large egg (1)

Directions :

1. Set the Air Fryer at 390° Fahrenheit.

2. Pour boiling water into the Air Fryer basket.

3. Break the egg into a dish and slide it into the water. Set the basket into the fryer.

4. Set the timer for 3 minutes. When ready, scoop the poached egg into a plate using a slotted spoon.

5. Serve with a serving of toast to your liking.

4. Baked Apple & Walnuts

Servings Provided: 2

Ingredients :

Apple or pear (1 medium)

Chopped walnuts (2 tbsp.)

Raisins (2 tbsp.)

Light margarine (1.5 tsp. - melted)

Cinnamon (.25 tsp.)

Nutmeg (.25 tsp.)

Water (.25 cup)

Directions :

1. Set the Air Fryer temperature at 350° Fahrenheit.
2. Cut the apple/pear in half around the middle and spoon out some of the flesh.
3. Place the apple or pear in the pan (to fit in the Air Fryer).
4. In a small mixing container, combine the cinnamon, nutmeg, margarine, raisins, and walnuts.
5. Add the mixture into the centers of the fruit halves.
6. Pour water into the pan.
7. Air-fry for 20 minutes

CHAPTER 10:

Lunch Recipes

5. **Bourbon Bacon Burger**

Servings Provided: 2

Ingredients :

- Bourbon (1 tbsp.)
- Brown sugar (2 tbsp.)
- Maple bacon (3 strips - cut in half)
- Ground beef - 80% lean (.75 lb.)
- Minced onion (1 tbsp.)
- BBQ sauce (2 tbsp.)
- Salt (.5 tsp.)
- Freshly ground black pepper (as desired)
- Colby Jack/Monterey Jack (2 slices)
- Kaiser rolls (2)

6. Lettuce And Tomato

for serving

· For the Sauce:

· BBQ sauce (2 tbsp.)

· Mayonnaise (2 tbsp.)

· Ground paprika (.25 tsp.)

· Freshly cracked black pepper

Directions :

1. Warm the Air Fryer at 390° Fahrenheit and pour a little water into the bottom of the fryer drawer.

2. Combine the brown sugar and bourbon in a small bowl. Place the bacon strips in the fryer basket and brush with the brown sugar mixture. Air-fry for four minutes.

3. Flip the bacon over, and recoat using more brown sugar and air- fry for another 4 minutes until crispy.

4. Prepare the burgers. Combine the onion, ground beef, barbecue sauce, salt, and pepper in a large bowl. Shape the meat into two burgers.

5. Put the burgers in the Air Fryer basket and air-fry the burgers at 370° Fahrenheit for 15-20 minutes (15 minutes for rare to medium-rare or 20 minutes for well-done). Flip the burgers halfway through the cooking process.

6. Prepare the burger sauce by combining the BBQ sauce, mayonnaise, paprika, and freshly ground black pepper in a bowl.

7. When the burgers are cooked to your liking, top each patty with a slice of Colby Jack cheese and air-fry for an additional minute, or long enough to melt the cheese. (You might want to

pin the cheese slice to the burger with a toothpick to prevent it from blowing off in your air fryer.)

8. Spread the sauce on the inside of the Kaiser rolls, place the burgers on the rolls, top with the bourbon bacon, lettuce, and tomato and serve.

7.   Chicken Fried Rice

Servings Provided: 5-6

Ingredients :

· Packed cooked chicken (1 cup)

· Cold cooked white rice (3 cups)

· Frozen carrots and peas (1 cup)

· Vegetable oil (1 tbsp.)

· Soy sauce (6 tbsp.)

· Diced onion (.5 cup)

· Also Needed: 7 by 2-inch cake pan

Directions :

1. Set the Air Fryer at 360° Fahrenheit.

2. Cook and dice the chicken. Prepare the rice. Dice the onion.

3. Add the chilled rice, soy sauce, and oil into a mixing bowl. Stir well.

4. Toss in the onion, chicken, peas, and carrots. Combine the fixings in the Air Fryer and fry for 20 minutes.

5. Enjoy as a luncheon treat or serve as a side with your favorite dinner time meal.

CHAPTER 11:

Dinner Recipes

8.   Air Fried Beef & Potato

Servings Provided: 4

Ingredients :

Mashed potatoes (3 cups)

Ground beef (1 lb.)

Eggs (2)

Garlic powder (2 tbsp.)

Sour cream (1 cup)

Freshly cracked black pepper (as desired)

Salt (1 pinch)

Directions :

1. Set the Air Fryer to reach 390° Fahrenheit.
2. Combine all of the fixings in a mixing container. Scoop it into a heat-safe dish.
3. Arrange in the fryer to cook for two minutes.
4. Serve for lunch or a quick dinner.

9.   Beef & Bacon Taco Rolls

Servings Provided: 2

Ingredients :

Ground beef (2 cups)

Bacon bits (.5 cup)

Tomato salsa (1 cup)

Shredded Monterey Jack Cheese (1 cup)

As desired - with the beef taco spices:

Garlic powder

Chili powder

Black pepper

Turmeric coconut wraps/your choice (4)

Directions :

1. Warm the Air Fryer to reach 390° Fahrenheit.
2. Mix the beef and chosen spices, and add it to each of the fixings into the wraps.
3. Roll up the wraps and arrange them in the Air Fryer.
4. Set the timer for 15 minutes and serve.

10.   Beef Empanadas

Servings Provided: 4

Ingredients :

Onion (1 small)

Cloves of garlic (2)

Olive oil (1 tbsp.)

Ground beef (1 lb.)

Empanada shells (1 pkg.)

Green pepper (.5 of 1)

Cumin (.5 tsp.)

Tomato salsa (.25 cup)

Egg yolk (1)

Pepper and sea salt (to your liking)

Directions :

1. Peel and mince the garlic and onion. Deseed and dice the pepper.

2. Pour the oil to a skillet using the high-heat temperature setting.

3. Fry the ground beef until browned. Drain the grease and add the onions and garlic. Cook for 4 minutes. Combine the remainder of fixings (omitting the milk, egg, and shells for now). Cook using the low setting for 10 minutes.Make an egg wash with the yolk and milk.Add the meat to half of the rolled dough, brushing the edges with the wash. Fold it over and seal using a fork, brushing with the wash, and adding it to the basket.Continue the process until all are done. Set the timer for 10 minutes in the Air Fryer at 350° Fahrenheit. Serve.

CHAPTER 12:

Side Dish Recipes

11.   Air-Fried Okra

Servings Provided: 4

INGREDIENTS :

All-purpose flour (.25 cup)

Cornmeal (1 cup)

Large egg (1)

Okra pods (.5 lb)

Salt (as desired)

DIRECTIONS :

1. Set the Air Fryer to 400° Fahrenheit.

2. Whisk the egg in a shallow dish. Slice and stir in the okra.

3. Mix the cornmeal and flour in a gallon-size zipper plastic bag. Drop five slices of okra into the cornmeal mixture, zip the bag, and shake. Remove the breaded okra to a plate. Repeat with remaining okra slices.Place half of the breaded slices into the fryer basket and mist using the cooking spray. Set the timer for four minutes. Shake the basket and mist okra with cooking oil spray again. Cook another four minutes. Shake the basket one last time and cook for another two minutes. Remove the okra from the basket and salt to your liking.

4. Repeat with the remaining okra slices.

12.   Avocado & Bacon Fries

Servings Provided: 2

Ingredients :

Egg (1)

Almond flour (1 cup)

Bacon – cooked – small bits (4 strips)

Avocados (2 large)

For Frying: Olive oil

Directions :

1. Set the Air Fryer at 355° Fahrenheit.

2. Whisk the eggs in one container. Add the flour with the bacon in another.

3. Slice the avocado using lengthwise cuts. Dip into the eggs, then the flour mixture.

4. Drizzle oil in the fryer tray and cook for 10 minutes on each side or until they're the way you like them.

13. Battered Baby Ears Of Corn

Servings Provided: 4

Ingredients :

Carom seeds (.5 tsp.)

Almond flour (1 cup)

Chili powder (.25 tsp.)

Garlic powder (1 tsp.)

Boiled baby ears of corn (4)

Baking soda (1 pinch)

Salt (to your liking)

Directions :

1. Warm the Air Fryer to reach 350° Fahrenheit.

2. Whisk the flour, salt, garlic powder, baking soda, chili powder, and carom seeds. Pour a little water into a bowl to make a batter. Dip the boiled corn in the mixture and arrange it in a foil-lined fryer basket. Set the timer for 10 minutes.

3. Serve with your favorite entrée.

14. Breaded Avocado Fries

Servings Provided: 2

Ingredients :

Large avocado (1)

Breadcrumbs (.5 cup)

Egg (1)

Salt (.5 tsp.)

Directions :

1. Warm the Air Fryer to reach 390° Fahrenheit.
2. Peel, remove the pit, and slice the avocado.
3. Prepare two shallow dishes, one with the breadcrumbs and salt, and one with a whisked egg.
4. Dip the avocado into the egg – then the breadcrumbs.
5. Add to the Air Fryer for ten minutes.
6. Serve as a side dish or an appetizer.

15.   Brussels Sprouts

Servings Provided: 4-5

Ingredients :

- Olive oil (5 tbsp.)
- Fresh brussels sprouts (1 lb.)
- Kosher salt (.5 tsp.)

Directions :

1. Prep the vegetables. Trim the stems and discard any damaged outer leaves. Cut into halves, rinse, and pat dry. Toss with the oil and salt.
2. Set the fryer temperature ahead of time to 390° Fahrenheit.
3. Toss the sprouts into the basket and air-fry for 15 minutes.
4. Shake the basket to ensure even browning.

16.   Buffalo Cauliflower

Servings Provided: 4

Ingredients :

Breadcrumbs (1 cup)

Cauliflower florets (4 cups)

Buffalo sauce (.25 cup)

Melted butter (.25 cup)

For the Dip: Your preferred dressing

Directions :

1. Melt the butter in a microwaveable dish. Whisk in the buffalo sauce.

2. Dip the florets in the butter mixture. Use the stem as a handle, holding it over a cup and let the excess drip away.

3. Dredge the florets through the breadcrumbs. Drop them into the Air Fryer. Set the timer for 14 to 17 minutes at 350° Fahrenheit. (The unit will not need to preheat since it is calculated into the time.)

4. Shake the basket several times during the cooking process. Serve alongside your favorite dip, making sure to eat it right away because the crunchiness goes away quickly.

Cooking Note: Reheat in the oven. Don't use the microwave or it will be mushy

CHAPTER 13:

Vegetarian Recipes

17.   Tasty Hasselback Potatoes

Preparation time: 10 minutes Cooking time: 45 minutes

Serve: 4

INGREDIENTS

4 potatoes wash and dry

1 tbsp. Dried thyme

1 tbsp. Dried rosemary

1 tbsp. Dried parsley

½ cup butter, melted

Pepper

Salt

DIRECTIONS

1. Place potato in hassel back slicer and slice potato using a sharp knife. In a small bowl, mix together melted butter, thyme, rosemary, parsley, pepper, and salt.

3. Rub melted butter mixture over potatoes and arrange potatoes on air fryer oven tray.

4. Bake potatoes at 350 f for 25 minutes.

NUTRITION: Calories: 356 Cal Total Fat: 23.4 g Saturated Fat: 0 g Cholesterol: 61 mg Sodium: 0 mg Total Carbs : 34.5 g Fiber: 0 g Sugar: 2.5 g Protein: 0 g

18.   Honey Sriracha Brussels Sprouts

Preparation time: 10 minutes

Cooking time: 15 minutes

Serve: 4

INGREDIENTS

½ lb. Brussels sprouts, cut stems then cut each in half

1 tbsp. Olive oil - ½ tsp salt

For sauce:

1 tbsp. Sriracha sauce

1 tbsp. Vinegar

1 tbsp. Lemon juice - 2 tsp Sugar

1 tbsp. Honey - 1 tsp garlic, minced

½ tsp olive oil

DIRECTIONS

1. Add all sauce Ingredients into the small saucepan and heat over low

heat for 2-3 minutes or until thickened.

2. Remove saucepan from heat and set aside.

3. Add brussels sprouts, oil, and salt in a zip-lock bag and shake well.

4. Transfer brussels sprouts on air fryer oven tray and air fry at 390 f

for 15 minutes. Shake halfway through.

5. Transfer brussels sprouts to the mixing bowl. Drizzle with sauce and toss until well coated.

NUTRITION: Calories: 86 Cal Total Fat: 4.3 g Saturated Fat: 0 g Cholesterol: 0 mg Sodium: 0 mg Total Carbs : 11.8 g Fiber: 0 g Sugar: 0g Protein: 2 g

19.   Roasted Carrots

Preparation time: 10 minutes

Cooking time: 20 minutes

Serve: 6

INGREDIENTS

2 lbs. Carrots, peeled, slice in half again slice half

2 ½ tbsp. Dried parsley

1 tsp dried oregano

1 tsp dried thyme

3 tbsp. Olive oil

Pepper

Salt

DIRECTIONS

1. Add carrots in a mixing bowl. Add remaining Ingredients on top of carrots and toss well.

2. Arrange carrots on air fryer oven pan and roast at 400 f for 10 minutes.

3. After 10 minutes turn carrots slices to the other side and roast for 10 minutes more

NUTRITION: Calories: 124 Cal Total Fat: 7.1 g Saturated Fat: 0 g Cholesterol: 0 mg Sodium: 0 mg Total Carbs : 15.3 g Fiber: 0 g Sugar: 7.5

g Protein: 0 g

CHAPTER 14:

Vegan Recipes

20.   Carrot Mix

Servings Provided: 4

Nutritional Facts Per Serving:

Protein Count: 3 grams

Net Carbohydrates: 4 grams

Total Fat Content: 7 grams

Calorie Count: 202

Ingredients :

Coconut milk (2 cups)

Steel-cut oats (.5 cup)

Shredded carrots (1 cup)

Agave nectar (.5 tsp.)

Ground cardamom (1 tsp.)

Saffron (1 pinch)

Directions :

1   Lightly spritz the Air Fryer pan using a cooking oil spray.

2   Warm the fryer to reach 365° Fahrenheit.

3   When it's hot, whisk and add the fixings (omit the saffron).

4   Set the timer for 15 minutes.

5   After the timer buzzes, portion into the serving dishes with a sprinkle of saffron.

CHAPTER 15:

Ketogenic Air Fried Specialties

21.   Air Bread & Egg Butter

For the Bread Servings Provided: 19

Nutritional Facts Per Serving:

Protein Count: 1.2 grams

Net Carbohydrates: 0.5 grams

Total Fat Content: 3.9 grams

Calorie Count: 40

Ingredients :

Eggs (3)

Baking powder (1 tsp.)

Sea salt (.25 tsp.)

Almond flour (1 cup)

Unchilled butter (.25 cup)

Directions :

Set the Air Fryer at 350° Fahrenheit.Whisk the eggs with a hand mixer. Mix in the rest of the fixings to make a dough. Knead the dough and cover using a tea towel for about ten minutes.Air-fry the bread 15 minutes. Remove the bread and let it cool down on a wooden board.Slice and serve with your favorite meal or as it is with butter (below).

CHAPTER 16:

Poultry Recipes

22.   BBQ Chicken – Gluten-Free

Servings Provided: 4

Ingredients :

Boneless – skinless chicken breast (2 large)

Seasoned flour/Gluten-free seasoned flour (.5 cup)

Barbecue sauce (1 cup)

Olive oil cooking spray

Directions :

1. Heat the Air Fryer to 390° Fahrenheit.Chop the chicken into bite-size chunks and place in a mixing bowl. Coat with the seasoned flour.

2. Lightly spritz the basket of the Air Fryer with olive oil cooking spray and evenly pour the chicken into the cooker.

3. Set the timer for 8 minutes.Open the Air Fryer, coat with olive oil spray, and flip the chicken as needed.Air-fry the chicken for eight more minutes.Be sure its internal reading is at least 165° Fahrenheit.Place the chicken into a dish and add the sauce to cover. Line the Air Fryer with a sheet of foil or add the chicken back to the fryer and cook for another 3 minutes until the sauce is warmed and the chicken is a bit more crispy and coated. Serve.

23.   Buffalo Chicken Wings

Servings Provided: 2-3

Ingredients :

Chicken wings (5 – trombo. 14 oz.)

Salt & black pepper (as desired)

Cayenne pepper (2 tsp. or to taste)

Red hot sauce (2 tbsp.)

Melted butter (1 tbsp.)

Optional: Garlic powder (.5 tsp.)

Directions :

1. Heat the Air Fryer temperature to reach 356° Fahrenheit.

2. Slice the wings into three sections (end tip, middle joint, and drumstick). Pat each one thoroughly dry using a paper towel.

3. Combine the pepper, salt, garlic powder, and cayenne pepper on a platter. Lightly cover the wings with the powder.

4. Arrange the chicken onto the wire rack and bake for 15 minutes, turning once at 7 minutes.

5. Combine the hot sauce with the melted butter in a dish to garnish the baked chicken when it is time to be served.

24.   Chicken Breast Tenderloins

Servings Provided: 4

Ingredients :

Butter/vegetable oil (2 tbsp.)

Breadcrumbs (3.33 tbsp.)

Egg (1)

Chicken tenderloins (8)

Directions :

1. Heat the Air Fryer temperature to 356° Fahrenheit.
2. Combine the breadcrumbs and oil – stirring until the mixture crumbles.
3. Whisk the egg and dredge the chicken through the egg, shaking off the excess.
4. Dip each piece of chicken into the crumbs and evenly coat.
5. Set the timer for 12 minutes.

25. Chicken Curry

Servings Provided: 4

Ingredients :

Chicken breast (1 lb.)

Olive oil (1 tsp.)

Onion (1)

Garlic (2 tsp.)

Lemongrass (1 tbsp.)

Chicken stock (.5 cup)

Apple cider vinegar (1 tbsp.)

Coconut milk (.5 cup)

Curry paste (2 tbsp.)

Directions :

1. Warm the fryer to reach 365° Fahrenheit.
2. Dice the chicken into cubes. Peel and dice the onion and combine in the Air Fryer basket. Cook for five minutes.
3. Remove the basket and add the rest of the fixings. Mix well and air-fry for ten more minutes.
4. Serve for a quick and easy meal.

26.   Chicken Fillet Strips

Servings Provided: 4

Ingredients :

Chicken fillets (1 lb.)

Paprika (1 tsp.)

Heavy cream (1 tbsp.)

Salt & pepper (.5 tsp.)

Butter (as needed)

Directions :

1.   Heat the Air Fryer at 365° Fahrenheit.

2.   Slice the fillets into strips and dust with salt and pepper.

3.   Add a light coating of butter to the basket.

4.   Arrange the strips in the basket and air-fry for six minutes.

5.   Flip the strips and continue frying for another five minutes.

6.   When done, garnish with the cream and paprika. Serve warm.

CHAPTER 17:

Seafood Recipes

27.   Air Fried Cod With Basil Vinaigrette

Preparation time: 0 minutes

Cooking time: 15 minutes

Servings: *4*

INGREDIENTS

¼ cup olive oil

4 cod fillets

A bunch of basil, torn

Juice from 1 lemon, freshly squeezed

Salt and pepper *to taste*

DIRECTIONS

1. Preheat the air fryer for 5 minutes.

2. Season the cod fillets with salt and pepper to taste.

3. Place in the air fryer and cook for 15 minutes at 3500f.

4. Meanwhile, mix the rest of the Ingredients in a bowl and toss to combine.

5. Serve the air fried cod with the basil vinaigrette.

CALORIES NUTRITION: 235; Carbohydrates: 1.9g; Protein: 14.3g; Fat: 18.9g

28.   Almond Flour Coated Crispy Shrimps

Preparation time: 0 minutes

Cooking time: 10 minutes

Servings: 4

INGREDIENTS

½ cup almond flour

1 tablespoon yellow mustard

1-pound raw shrimps, peeled and deveined

3 tablespoons olive oil

Salt and pepper to taste

DIRECTIONS

1. Place all Ingredients in a ziploc bag and give a good shake.

2. Place in the air fryer and cook for 10 minutes at 4000f.

NUTRITION: 206; Carbohydrates: 1.3g; Protein: 23.5g; Fat: 11.9g

29.   Apple Slaw Topped Alaskan Cod Filet

Preparation time: 0 minutes

Servings: 3

Cooking time: 15 minutes

INGREDIENTS

¼ cup mayonnaise

½ red onion, diced

1 ½ pounds frozen alaskan cod

1 box whole wheat panko breadcrumbs

1 granny smith apple, julienned

1 tablespoon vegetable oil

1 teaspoon paprika

2 cups napa cabbage, shredded

Salt and pepper to taste

DIRECTIONS

1. Preheat the air fryer to 390of.

2. Place the grill pan accessory in the air fryer.

3. Brush the fish with oil and dredge in the breadcrumbs.

4. Place the fish on the grill pan and cook for 15 minutes. Make sure to flip the fish halfway through the Cooking time.

5. Meanwhile, prepare the slaw by mixing the remaining Ingredients in a bowl.

6. Serve the fish with the slaw.

NUTRITION: 316; Carbs : 13.5g; Protein: 37.8g; Fat: 12.2g

30.   Baked Cod Fillet Recipe From Thailand

Preparation time: 0 minutes

Cooking time: 20 minutes

Servings: 4

INGREDIENTS

¼ cup coconut milk, freshly squeezed

1 tablespoon lime juice, freshly squeezed

1-pound cod fillet, cut into bite-sized pieces

Salt and pepper to taste

DIRECTIONS

1. Preheat the air fryer for 5 minutes.

2. Place all Ingredients in a baking dish that will fit in the air fryer.

3. Place in the air fryer.

4. Cook for 20 minutes at 3250f.

NUTRITION: 844; Carbohydrates: 2.3g; Protein: 21.6g; Fat: 83.1g

CHAPTER 18:

Meat Recipes

31. Pork And Mixed Greens Salad

Preparation time: 10 minutes

Cooking time: 15 minutes

Servings: 4

INGREDIENTS

2 pounds pork tenderloin, cut into 1-inch slices

1 teaspoon olive oil

1 teaspoon dried marjoram

⅛ teaspoon freshly ground black pepper

6 cups mixed salad greens

1 red bell pepper, sliced

1 (8-ounce) package button mushrooms, sliced

⅓ cup low-Sodium low-Fat vinaigrette dressing

DIRECTIONS

1. In a medium bowl, mix the pork slices and olive oil. Toss to coat.

2. Sprinkle with the marjoram and pepper and rub these into the pork.

3. Grill the pork in the air fryer, in batches, for about 4 to 6 minutes, or until the pork reaches at least 145°f on a meat thermometer.

4. Meanwhile, in a serving bowl, mix the salad greens, red bell pepper, and mushrooms. Toss gently.

5. When the pork is cooked, add the slices to the salad. drizzle with the vinaigrette and toss gently. Serve immediately.

NUTRITION: Calories: 172; Fat: 5 g (26% ofCalories from Fat); saturated

Fat: 1g; Protein: 27g; Carbohydrates: 28g; Sodium: 124mg; Fiber: 2g;

32.   Pork Satay

Preparation time: 15 minutes

Cooking time: 9 to 14 minutes

Servings: 4

INGREDIENTS

1 (1-pound) pork tenderloin, cut into 1½-inch cubes

¼ cup minced onion

2 garlic cloves, minced

1 jalapeño pepper, minced

2 tablespoons freshly squeezed lime juice

2 tablespoons coconut milk

2 tablespoons unsalted peanut butter

2 teaspoons curry powder

DIRECTIONS

1. In a medium bowl, mix the pork, onion, garlic, jalapeño, lime juice, coconut milk, peanut butter, and curry powder until well combined. Let stand for 10 minutes at room temperature.

2. With a slotted spoon, remove the pork from the marinade. Reserve the marinade.

3. Thread the pork onto about 8 bamboo or metal skewers. Grill for 9 to 14 minutes, brushing once with the reserved marinade, until the pork reaches at least 145°f on a meat thermometer. Discard any remaining marinade. Serve immediately.

NUTRITION: Calories: 194; Fat: 7g (32% ofCalories from Fat); saturated

Fat: 3g; Protein: 25g; Carbohydrates: 7g; Sodium: 65mg; Fiber: 1g

33. Crispy Mustard Pork Tenderloin

Preparation time: 10 minutes

Cooking time: 12 to 16 minutes

Servings: 4

INGREDIENTS

3 tablespoons low-Sodium grainy mustard

2 teaspoons olive oil

¼ teaspoon dry mustard powder

1 (1-pound) pork tenderloin, silver skin and excess Fat trimmed and discarded

2 slices low-Sodium whole-wheat bread, crumbled

¼ cup ground walnuts

2 tablespoons cornstarch

DIRECTIONS

1. In a small bowl, stir together the mustard, olive oil, and mustard powder. Spread this mixture over the pork.

2. On a plate, mix the breadcrumbs, walnuts, and cornstarch. Dip the mustard-coated pork into the crumb mixture to coat.

3. Air-fry the pork for 12 to 16 minutes, or until it registers at least 145°f on a meat thermometer. Slice to serve.

NUTRITION: Calories: 239; Fat: 9g (34% ofCalories from Fat); saturated

Fat: 2g; Protein: 26g; Carbohydrates: 15g; Sodium: 118mg; Fiber: 2g

34. Apple Pork Tenderloin

Preparation time: 10 minutes

Cooking time: 14 to 19 minutes

Servings: 4

INGREDIENTS

1 (1-pound) pork tenderloin, cut into 4 pieces

1 tablespoon apple butter

2 teaspoons olive oil

2 granny smith apples or jonagold apples, sliced

3 celery stalks, sliced

1 onion, sliced

½ teaspoon dried marjoram

⅓ cup apple juice

DIRECTIONS

1. Rub each piece of pork with the apple butter and olive oil.

2. In a medium metal bowl, mix the pork, apples, celery, onion, marjoram, and apple juice.

3. Place the bowl into the air fryer and roast for 14 to 19 minutes, or until the pork reaches at least 145°f on a meat thermometer and the apples and vegetables are tender. Stir once during Cooking . Serve immediately.

NUTRITION: Calories: 213; Fat: 5g (21% ofCalories from Fat); saturated

Fat: 1g; Protein: 24g; Carbohydrates: 20g; Sodium: 88mg; Fiber: 3g

35. Fried Pork With Sweet And Sour Glaze

Preparation time: 5 minutes Cooking time: 30 minutes

Servings: 4

INGREDIENTS

¼ cup rice wine vinegar

¼ teaspoon chinese five spice powder

1 cup potato starch

1 green onion, chopped

2 large eggs, beaten

2 pounds pork chops cut into chunks

2 tablespoons cornstarch + 3 tablespoons water

5 tablespoons brown Sugar

Salt and pepper to taste

DIRECTIONS

1. Preheat the air fryer oven to 390°f.

2. Season pork chops with salt and pepper to taste.

3. Dip the pork chops in egg. Set aside.

4. In a bowl, combine the potato starch and chinese five spice powder.

5. Dredge the pork chops in the flour mixture.

6. Place in the double layer rack and cook for 30 minutes.

7. Meanwhile, place the vinegar and brown Sugar in a saucepan. Season with salt and pepper to taste. Stir in the cornstarch slurry and allow to simmer until thick.

8. Serve the pork chops with the sauce and garnish with green onions.

NUTRITION: Calories: 420; Fat: 11.8g; Protein:69.2g

36.   Oregano-Paprika On Breaded Pork

Preparation time: 10 minutes

Cooking time: 30 minutes

Servings: 4

INGREDIENTS

¼ cup water

¼ teaspoon dry mustard

½ teaspoon black pepper

½ teaspoon cayenne pepper

½ teaspoon garlic powder

½ teaspoon salt

1 cup panko breadcrumbs

1 egg, beaten

2 teaspoons oregano

4 lean pork chops

4 teaspoons paprika

DIRECTIONS

1. Preheat the air fryer oven to 390°f.

2. Pat dry the pork chops.

3. In a mixing bowl, combine the egg and water. Then set aside.

4. In another bowl, combine the rest of the Ingredients.

5. Dip the pork chops in the egg mixture and dredge in the flour mixture.

6. Place in the air fryer basket and cook for 25 to 30 minutes until golden.

NUTRITION: Calories: 364; Fat: 20.2g; Protein:42.9g

CHAPTER 19:

Dessert Recipe

37.   Air Fried Plantains

Servings Provided: 4

Ingredients :

Avocado or sunflower oil (2 tsp.)

Ripened/almost brown – plantains (2)

Optional: Salt (.125 tsp.)

Directions :

1. Warm up the Air Fryer to 400° Fahrenheit.

2. Slice the plantains at an angle for a .5-inch thickness.

3. Mix the oil, salt, and plantains in a container – making sure you coat the surface thoroughly.

4. Set the timer for eight to ten minutes; shake after five minutes. If they are not done to your liking, add a minute or two more.

38.   Air Fryer Beignets

Servings Provided: 7

Ingredients :

All-purpose flour (.5 cup)

White sugar (.25 cup)

Water (.125 cup)

Large egg (1 separated)

Melted butter (1.5 tsp.)

Baking powder (.5 tsp.)

Vanilla extract (.5 tsp.)

Salt (1 pinch)

Confectioners' sugar (2 tbsp.)

Also Needed: Silicone egg-bite mold

Directions :

1.   Warm the Air Fryer to reach 370° Fahrenheit. Spray the using a nonstick cooking spray.

2.   Whisk the flour, sugar, water, egg yolk, butter, baking powder, vanilla extract, and salt together in a large mixing bowl. Stir to combine.

3.   Using an electric hand mixer (medium speed), mix the egg white in a small bowl until soft peaks form. Fold into the

4.   batter. Pour the mixture into the mold using a small hinged ice cream scoop.

5.   Arrange the filled silicone mold in the basket of the Air Fryer.

6. Cook for 10 minutes. Remove mold from the basket carefully, pop the beignets out, and flip them over onto a parchment paper-lined round.

7. Place the parchment round with beignets back into the fryer basket. Cook for another 4 minutes.

8. Remove the beignets from the Air Fryer basket and dust with confectioners' sugar.

9. mold

39.   Banana Smores

Servings Provided: 4

Ingredients :

Bananas (4)

Mini-peanut butter chips (3 tbsp.)

Graham cracker cereal (3 tbsp.)

Mini-semi-sweet chocolate chips (3 tbsp.)

Directions :

1.   Heat the Air Fryer in advance to 400° Fahrenheit.

2.   Slice the un-peeled bananas lengthwise along the inside of the curve. Don't slice through the bottom of the peel. Open slightly - forming a pocket.

3.   Fill each pocket with chocolate chips, peanut butter chips, and marshmallows. Poke the cereal into the filling.

4.   Arrange the stuffed bananas in the fryer basket, keeping them upright with the filling facing up.

5.   Air-fry until the peel has blackened, and the chocolate and marshmallows have toasted (6 minutes).

6.   Cool for 1-2 minutes. Spoon out the filling to serve.

40.   Blackberry & Apricot Crumble

Servings Provided: 6

Ingredients :

Fresh blackberries (5.5 oz.)

Lemon juice (2 tbsp.)

Fresh apricots (18 oz.)

Sugar (.5 cup)

Salt (1 pinch)

Flour (1 cup)

Cold butter (5 tbsp.)

Directions :

1.   Heat the Air Fryer to 390° Fahrenheit.

2.   Lightly grease an 8-inch oven dish with a spritz of cooking oil.

3.   Remove the stones, cut the apricots into cubes, and put them in a container.

4.   Combine the lemon juice, blackberries, and two tablespoons of sugar with the apricots and mix. Place the fruit in the oven dish.

5.   Combine the salt, remainder of the sugar, and flour in a mixing container. Add one tablespoon of cold water and the butter, using your fingertips to make a crumbly mixture.

6.   Crumble the mixture over the fruit, pressing them down.

7.   Place the dish in the basket and slide it into the Air Fryer. Fry for 20 minutes. It is ready when it is cooked thoroughly, and the top is browned.

41.   Sweet Squares

Preparation time: 10 minutes

Cooking time: 30 minutes

Servings: 6

INGREDIENTS

1 cup flour

½ cup butter, soft

1 cup Sugar

¼ cup powdered Sugar

2 teaspoons lemon peel, grated

2 tablespoons lemon juice

2 eggs, whisked

½ teaspoon baking powder

DIRECTIONS

1. In a bowl, mix flour with powdered Sugar and butter, stir well, press on the bottom of a pan that fits your air fryer, introduce in the fryer and bake at 350 degrees f for 14 minutes.

2. In another bowl, mix Sugar with lemon juice, lemon peel, eggs and baking powder, stir using your mixer and spread over baked crust.

3. Bake for 15 minutes more, leave aside to cool down, cut into medium squares and serve cold.

4. Enjoy!

NUTRITION: Calories 100, Fat 4, Fiber 1, Carbs12, Protein 1

42.   Plum Bars

Preparation time: 10 minutes

Cooking time: 16 minutes

Servings: 8

INGREDIENTS

2 cups dried plums

6 tablespoons water

2 cup rolled oats

1 cup brown Sugar

½ teaspoon baking soda

1 teaspoon cinnamon powder

2 tablespoons butter, melted

1 egg, whisked

Cooking spray

DIRECTIONS

1. In your food processor, mix plums with water and blend until you obtain a sticky spread.

2. In a bowl, mix oats with cinnamon, baking soda, Sugar, egg and butter and whisk really well.

3. Press half of the oats mix in a baking pan that fits your air fryer sprayed with Cooking oil, spread plums mix and top with the other half of the oats mix.

4. Introduce in your air fryer and cook at 350 degrees f for 16 minutes.

5. Leave mix aside to cool down, cut into medium bars and serve.

6. Enjoy!

NUTRITION: Calories 111, Fat 5, Fiber 6, Carbs12, Protein 6

43. Brown Butter Cookies

Preparation time: 10 minutes

Cooking time: 10 minutes

Servings: 6

INGREDIENTS

1 and ½ cups butter

2 cups brown Sugar

2 eggs, whisked

3 cups flour

2/3 cup pecans, chopped

2 teaspoons vanilla extract

1 teaspoon baking soda

½ teaspoon baking powder

DIRECTIONS

1. Heat up a pan with the butter over medium heat, stir until it melts, add brown Sugar and stir until these dissolves.

2. In a bowl, mix flour with pecans, vanilla extract, baking soda, baking powder and eggs and stir well.

3. Add brown butter, stir well and arrange spoonful of this mix on a lined baking sheet that fits your air fryer.

4. Introduce in the fryer and cook at 340 degrees f for 10 minutes.

5. Leave cookies to cool down and serve.

6. Enjoy!

NUTRITION: Calories 144, Fat 5, Fiber 6, Carbs19, Protein 2

44.   Sweet Potato Cheesecake

Preparation time: 10 minutes

Cooking time: 5 minutes

Servings: 4

INGREDIENTS

4 tablespoons butter, melted

6 ounces mascarpone, soft

8 ounces cream cheese, soft

2/3 cup graham crackers, crumbled

¾ cup milk

1 teaspoon vanilla extract

2/3 cup sweet potato puree

¼ teaspoons cinnamon powder

DIRECTIONS

1. In a bowl, mix butter with crumbled crackers, stir well, press on the

bottom of a cake pan that fits your air fryer and keep in the fridge for now.

2. In another bowl, mix cream cheese with mascarpone, sweet potato puree, milk, cinnamon and vanilla and whisk really well.

3. Spread this over crust, introduce in your air fryer, cook at 300 degrees f for 4 minutes and keep in the fridge for a few hours before serving.

4. Enjoy!

NUTRITION: Calories 172, Fat 4, Fiber 6, Carbs8, Protein 3

CHAPTER 20:

The Best Recipes Ever

45.   Roasted Cauliflower With Nuts & Raisins

Preparation time: 0 minutes

Cooking time: 15 minutes

Servings: 4

INGREDIENTS

1 small cauliflower head, cut into florets

2 tablespoons pine nuts, toasted

2 tablespoons raisins, soak in boiling water and drain

1 teaspoon curry powder

½ teaspoon sea salt

3 tablespoons olive oil

DIRECTIONS

1. Preheat your air fryer to 320°fahrenheit for 2-minutes. Add Ingredients into a bowl and toss to combine. Add the cauliflower mixture to air fryer basket and cook for 15-minutes.

NUTRITION: Calories: 264, total Fat: 26g, Carbs : 8g, Protein: 2g

CHAPTER 21:

Smart Ovenair Fryerrecipes

46.   Thyme Lamb Chops With Asparagus

Preparation time: 10 minutes Cooking time: 20 minutes Servings: 4

Ingredients:

1 pound lamb chops 2tspolive oil

1½ tsp chopped fresh thyme 1 garlic clove, minced

Salt and black pepper to taste 4 asparagus spears, trimmed

Directions: Preheat your air fryer to 400 f. Spray the air fryer basket with cooking spray.

Drizzle the asparagus with some olive oil, sprinkle with salt, and set aside. Season the lamb with salt and black pepper. Brush with the remaining olive oil and transfer to the cooking basket. Cook for 10minutes, slide out the basket, turn the chops and add the asparagus. Cook for another 5 minutes. Serve sprinkled with thyme.

Nutrition: Calories: 371.9 kcal Total fat:22.1 g

Saturated fat: 5.2 g Cholesterol:708.9 mg

Sodium: 111.2 mg

Total carbs: 6.2 g Fiber: 2.3 g Sugar: 0.4 g

Protein: 37.1 g

47. Garlic Lamb Chops With Thyme

Preparation time: 10 minutes Cooking time: 30 minutes Servings: 4

Ingredients:

4 lamb chops

garlic clove, peeled 1 tbsp plus

tsp olive oil

½ tbsp oregano

½ tbsp thyme

½ tsp salt

¼ tsp black pepper

Directions:

Preheat the air fryer to 390 f. Coat the garlic clove with 1 tsp. Of olive oil and place it in the air fryer for

10 minutes. Meanwhile, mix the herbs and seasonings with the remaining olive oil.

Using a towel or a mitten, squeeze the hot roasted garlic clove into the herb mixture and stir to combine.

Coat the lamb chops with the mixture well, and place in the air fryer. Cook for 8 to 12 minutes.

Nutrition: Calories: 177.4 kcal Total fat: 7.9 g Saturated fat: 2.6 g Cholesterol: 72.6 mg Sodium: 1236.4 mg Total

carbs: 1.7 g Fiber: 0.5 g Sugar: 0 g Protein: 23.4 g

48. Lamb Chops And Mint Sauce

Preparation time: 10 minutes Cooking time: 29 minutes Servings: 4

Ingredients:

8 lamb chops

1 cup mint; chopped 1 garlic clove; minced 2 tbsp. Olive oil

Juice of 1 lemon

A pinch of salt and black pepper

Directions:

In a blender, combine all the ingredients: except the lamb and pulse well.

Rub lamb chops with the mint sauce, put them in your air fryer's basket and cook at 400°f for 12 minutes on each side

Divide everything between plates and serve.

Nutrition: Calories: 284 kcal Total fat: 14 g Saturated fat: 0 g Cholesterol: 0 mg Sodium: 0 mg Total carbs: 6 g

Fiber: 3 g Sugar: 0 g Protein: 16 g

49. Garlic Infused Roast Beef

Servings: 10

Cooking Time: 75 Minutes

Ingredients:

3 lb. beef roast, room temperature 4 cloves garlic, cut in thin slivers Olive oil spray,

1 tsp salt

tsp pepper

tsp rosemary

Directions:

Trim off the fat from the roast. Use a sharp knife to pierce the roast in intervals,

½-inch deep. Insert garlic

sliver in holes, pushing into the meat.

Lightly spray the beef with oil and season with salt, pepper, and rosemary.

Place the baking pan in position 1 of the oven. Set to convection bake on 325°F for 60 minutes. Spray the fryer basket with oil and place roast in it. Once the oven has preheated for 5 minutes, place the

basket on the pan. Cook 60 minutes, or until beef reaches desired doneness.

Remove from oven and let rest 10 minutes. Slice thinly and serve.

Nutrition Info:Calories 265, Total Fat 13g, Saturated Fat 5g, Total Carbs 1g, Net Carbs 1g, Protein 36g, Sugar 0g,

Fiber 0g, Sodium 342mg, Potassium 478mg, Phosphorus 288mg

50. Caramelized Pork Shoulder

Servings: 8

Cooking Time: 20 Minutes

Ingredients:

1/3 cup soy sauce

2 tablespoons sugar

tablespoon honey

pound pork shoulder, cut into 1½-inch thick slices

Directions:

Preparing the Ingredients. In a bowl, mix together all ingredients except pork.

Add pork and coat with marinade generously.

Cover and refrigerate o marinate for about 2-8 hours.

Preheat the Breville Smart air fryer oven to 335 degrees F.

Air Frying. Place the pork in an Air fryer rack/basket.

Cook for about 10 minutes.

Now, set the Breville Smart air fryer oven to 390 degrees F. Cook for about 10 minutes.